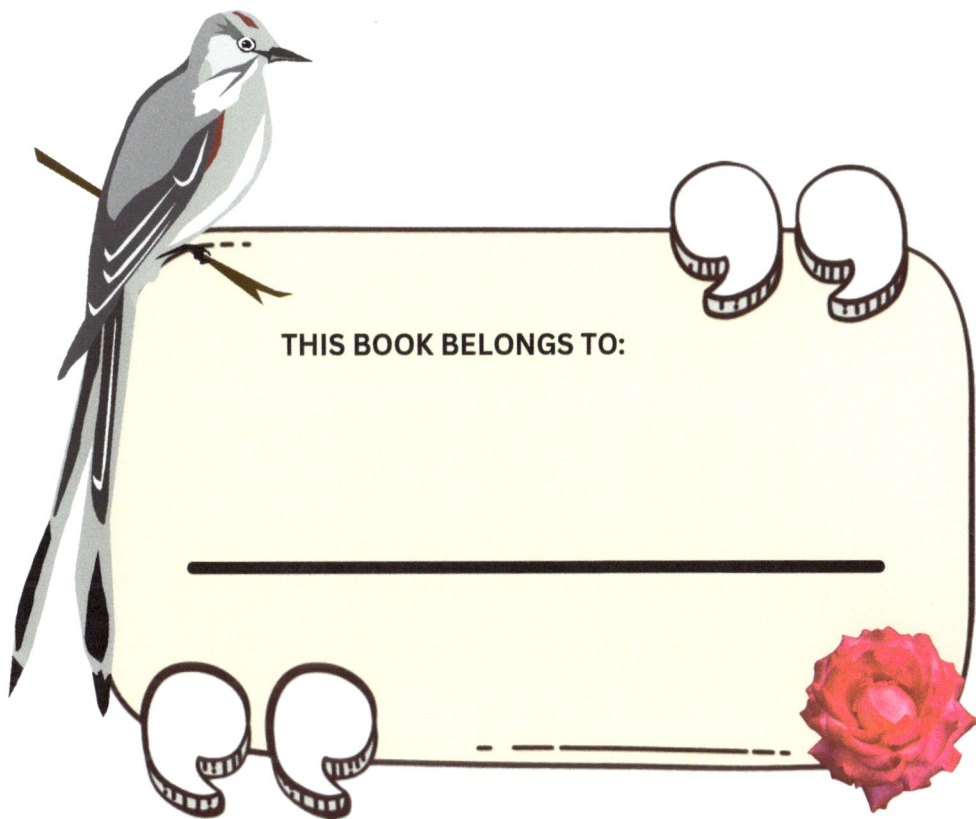

THIS BOOK BELONGS TO:

_____

WELCOME TO OKLAHOMA

Dedicated to all the explorers.

ISBN 978-1-958985-79-3

www.joeysavestheday.com

A Mimi Book

Oklahoma's name comes from the Choctaw language. It combines okla, meaning "people," and humma, meaning "red," so together it means "red people." The name was first suggested in 1866 by Choctaw Chief Allen Wright, and it was later chosen when Oklahoma became a state in 1907.

Oklahoma was the forty-sixth state to join the Union. It officially joined on November 16, 1907.

46th

Oklahoma is located in the South-Central region of the United States and is bordered by six states: Texas, Arkansas, Missouri, Kansas, Colorado, and New Mexico.

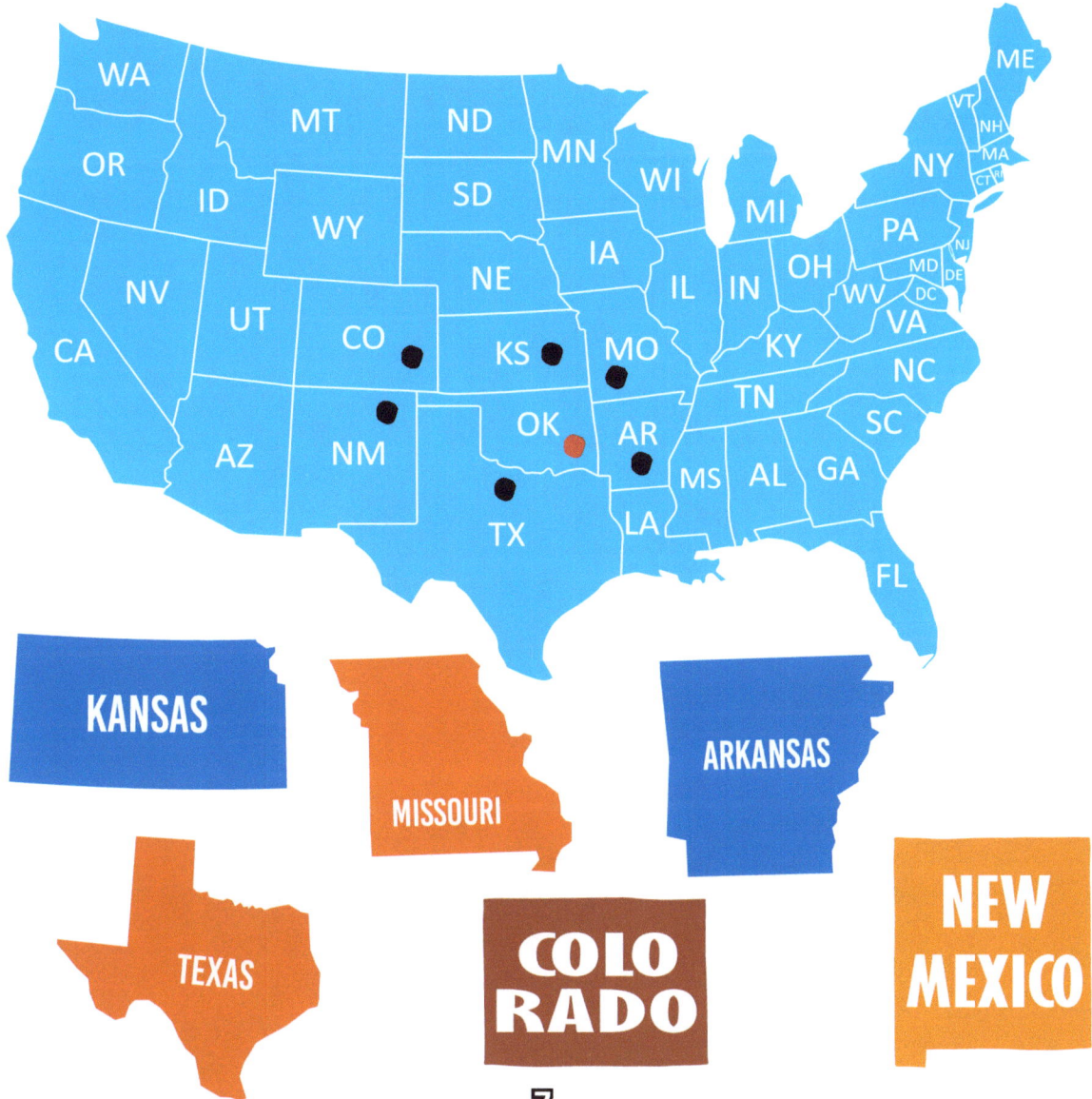

KANSAS

MISSOURI

ARKANSAS

TEXAS

COLO RADO

NEW MEXICO

Oklahoma City is the capital of Oklahoma. It officially became the capital on June 11, 1910.

Oklahoma City, Oklahoma, has an estimated population of about 712,900 people.

Oklahoma is the twentieth largest state in the United States by area.

Oklahoma

Bricktown, Oklahoma City

There are approximately 4,095,390 people residing in the state of Oklahoma.

Tulsa, Oklahoma

Carl Magee was an Oklahoma newspaperman who invented the first parking meter in 1935. His coin-operated device kept cars from staying too long in one spot, helping busy downtowns stay fair and organized.

Oklahoma is known for the fried onion burger. It started in the 1920s when cooks mixed thin-sliced onions into hamburger meat to save money. The onions cooked into the patty, making it sweet, crispy, and full of flavor. Today, it's a proud Oklahoma tradition, especially in the town of El Reno.

Oklahoma

There are 77 counties in Oklahoma.

Here is a list of twenty of those counties:

Atoka	Garfield	Nowata	Sequoyah
Beckham	Harper	Okmulgee	Tulsa
Bryan	Kiowa	Pawnee	Wagoner
Choctaw	Marshall	Roger Mills	Washita
Delaware	Murray	Seminole	Woodward

Guthrie Lake is a peaceful, man-made lake just outside the town of Guthrie. It was created by building a dam to collect water for the community, just like many of the more than 200 man-made lakes found across Oklahoma. Today, it's a calm place for fishing, boating, and family picnics, with a fishing dock, boat ramps, and plenty of space to enjoy the sunshine by the water.

MADE IN USA

Oklahoma is home to one of the largest Native American communities in the country. Today, 38 tribes have their headquarters in the state, each adding its own traditions, languages, and stories. Their cultures shape Oklahoma's identity and make it one of the most vibrant places in the United States.

The Pony Bridge, also called the Bridgeport Pony Bridge, is one of the most famous stops on Route 66. Built in 1933, it stretches almost a mile across the South Canadian River with 38 pony-truss spans that give it its nickname. After a big renovation, it reopened in 2024, welcoming travelers back to one of Oklahoma's classic Route 66 landmarks.

Natural Falls State Park sits in the rolling hills of northeast Oklahoma, where a tall 77-foot waterfall pours into a quiet, mossy canyon. The air feels cool and peaceful, even in summer. Families walk along short, easy trails to spot ferns, wildflowers, and tiny streams weaving through the forest. The park was once called Dripping Springs, and its beautiful scenery was even used in the movie Where the Red Fern Grows.

NATURAL

The Oklahoma state bird is the Scissor-tailed Flycatcher. It was chosen as the state bird on May 26, 1951.

OKLAHOMA

The official state flower of Oklahoma is the Oklahoma Rose. It was chosen as the state flower in 2004.

OFFICIAL

A couple of Oklahoma's nicknames include the Sooner State and the Boomer's Paradise.

Oklahoma's state motto, "Labor omnia vincit," meaning "Work Conquers All," was officially adopted in 1907.

WORK

ALL

OKLAHOMA
OKLAHOMA
OKLAHOMA
OKLAHOMA

The abbreviation for Oklahoma is OK.

OK

Oklahoma's state flag was officially adopted on April 2, 1925.

OKLAHOMA

Some crops grown in Oklahoma are corn, cotton, potatoes, and sweet potatoes.

Some animals that live in Oklahoma are black bears, bats, gray foxes, groundhogs, and rattle snakes.

Oklahoma experiences significant temperature fluctuations, ranging from very hot to very cold, depending on the time of year. The hottest temperature recorded in Oklahoma was 120 degrees Fahrenheit in Alva, Oklahoma, on July 18, 1936. The coldest temperature ever recorded in Oklahoma was -31 degrees (31 degrees below zero) Fahrenheit in Nowata, Oklahoma, on February 10, 2011.

Hot

Cold

ZOO

The Oklahoma City Zoo is located in the heart of Oklahoma City and is home to hundreds of animals from all around the world. Kids can see elephants, lions, giraffes, gorillas, rhinos, and playful monkeys, along with bright birds, reptiles, and even aquatic animals.

Turner Falls is one of Oklahoma's tallest and most famous waterfalls. It's located in the Arbuckle Mountains near the town of Davis, where Honey Creek drops 77 feet into a bright blue swimming hole. Families visit to see the waterfall, explore the rocky trails, and enjoy the cool water on hot days.

Will Rogers World Airport is the biggest airport in Oklahoma, and it sits on the southwest side of Oklahoma City, about six miles from downtown. Its address is 7100 Terminal Drive, Oklahoma City, Oklahoma. This busy airport helps people travel all over the country, with flights to places like Atlanta, Chicago, New York, and San Francisco. It's named after Will Rogers, a famous Oklahoma entertainer who loved to travel.

3 CENTS

"I NEVER MET A MAN I DIDN'T LIKE" – WILL ROGERS

UNITED STATES POSTAGE

The Oklahoma City Dodgers are a Triple-A baseball team based in Oklahoma City, right in the heart of the state. They play their home games at Chickasaw Bricktown Ballpark, a bright and lively stadium in the Bricktown entertainment district. As the top minor-league affiliate of the Los Angeles Dodgers, this team helps develop future major-league stars.

FOOTBALL

The Oklahoma Sooners are one of the most well-known college football teams in the country. They play in Norman, Oklahoma, at Gaylord Family-Oklahoma Memorial Stadium, a huge and energetic stadium filled with cheering fans dressed in crimson and cream. The Sooners have a long history of winning seasons, exciting games, and famous players who went on to the NFL.

The Eastern Redbud is Oklahoma's state tree. Every spring, it covers its branches with bright pink flowers that make the whole state look cheerful after winter. Its leaves are shaped like little green hearts, and the tree grows in forests, fields, and even along roadsides.

The White Bass is Oklahoma's state fish. It has a shiny silver body with dark stripes and loves to swim in big groups. Every spring, white bass travel up rivers in huge schools, making them fun and exciting for families to catch. Because they're strong swimmers and easy to spot during their spring run, the white bass has become one of Oklahoma's most popular and well-loved fish.

OKLAHOMA

Can you name these?

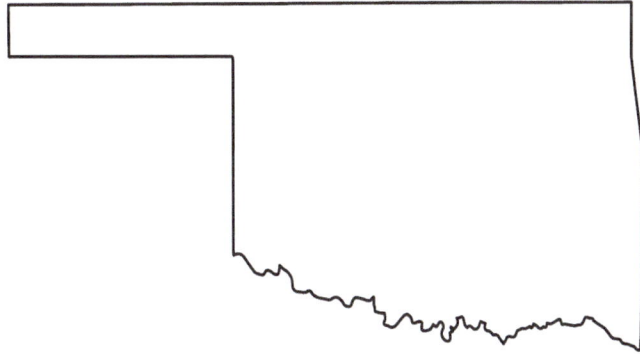

OKLAHOMA

I hope you enjoyed
learning about
Oklahoma.

To explore fun facts about the other 49 states,
visit my website at www.joeysavestheday.com.
You'll also find a wide variety of homeschool
resources to support joyful learning at home.
If you enjoyed this book, I would be grateful if
you left a review. Your feedback truly helps.
Thank you for your support!

TIME
TO SAY
GOODBYE

Check out these other interesting books in the Wonderful World of series!

OHIO FACTS

UTAH FACTS

TEXAS FACTS

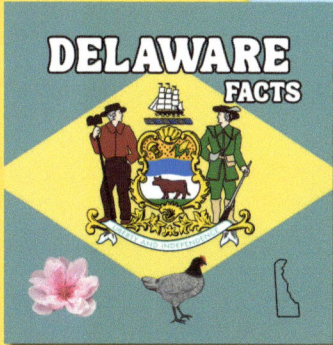
DELAWARE Facts

CALIFORNIA FACTS
CALIFORNIA REPUBLIC

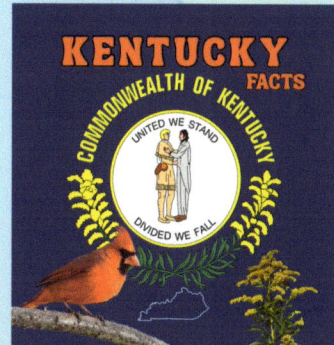
KENTUCKY FACTS
COMMONWEALTH OF KENTUCKY
UNITED WE STAND
DIVIDED WE FALL

GEORGIA FACTS

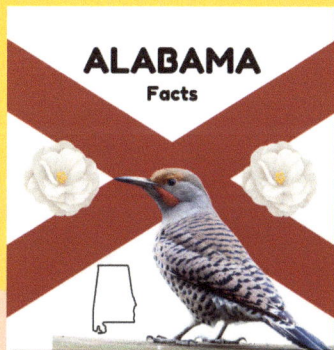
ALABAMA Facts

Alaska Facts

www.mimibooks.com

www.ingramcontent.com/pod-product-compliance
Lightning Source LLC
Chambersburg PA
CBHW041549040426
42447CB00002B/110